# THE RIVER OF LIFE

*Poems for the Main Events
in Our Journey*

*by*

George A. Doyle

DORRANCE PUBLISHING CO., INC.
PITTSBURGH, PENNSYLVANIA 15222

ISBN # 0-8059-3608-4
Printed in the United States of America

*First Printing*


For information or to order additional books, please write:
Dorrance Publishing Co., Inc.
643 Smithfield Street
Pittsburgh, Pennsylvania 15222
U.S.A.

To Life

To Love

and

To the Women

who have been both

to me.

## The River's Tale

Life is a Journey on a Great River
   with countless other
   fellow-travelers.
Each of us finds there is
   a time for all things—
a time for happiness, a time
  for sadness—
    a time for love, a time
        for loss of love—
    a time for work, a time
        for rest—
    a time for war, a time
        for peace—
    a time for life, a time
        for death—
Yet always there is a time
        for rebirth.
Let me tell you of my times,
   and you may find
      your tale
  on the River of Life.

# Contents

*Section I*

*When a Beloved Dies*

## My Beloved Died

*Yes,*
*my beloved died.*
*The beautiful flower*
*I held in my hands*
*withered suddenly*
*and died.*
*No, was killed really*
*—by an evil,*
*monstrous thing inside.*
*I took her home*
*from across the world.*
*Twenty-five days*
*were all she had,*
*and she lived them graciously.*
*In control of all*
*till the last hour,*
*when her children*
*gathered,*
*prayed round her bed,*
*escorted her*
*to her God,*
*Who must love her*
*as we have loved her.*

# Her Hands

They were small
  and warm
  and did beautiful things beautifully,
  but oh how they could work
    at the things of earth.
They touched you
  and your heart soared,
  made you feel good inside.
Yet,
    they washed the clothes
    and wrung them drier than ever I could,
    scrubbed the floor,
    did the ironing,
    polished the silver,
    drove the car,
    planted flowers,
    washed babies, so many babies,
      —eight, you know.
And in the end,
  took my head,
  one hand on each side,
  and blessed me.
I can never forget
  the surge of spirit
  that poured into me,
  took over my soul.
I told her
  I can feel God
    through your hands.
  I know already
    God is in this house.
And we both knew
  soon the hands
  would be gone from me.

# Is Your Beloved dying?

You have known it for many days
and you do your chores,
of course, you must.

Day after day now
she watches, waits.
She asks you, "How long?" It hurts you.

She must not die
in a hospital.
That's cruel, horrid banishment.

Go see to it, as you must,
that she can live
her last days in her home.

Tell her over and over
you love her more now
than ever you could.

Thank her for all,
for having made what she did of you.
She did, you know.

Surround her with Peace,
with all the Love you can gather.
Soon she'll be gone.

In her last moments
help her to welcome Death.
Escort her to her God.

We had the privilege,
her children and I,
when My Beloved died.

# Is This Your Last Day?

*You don't know, of course,*
*unless you knew you would die soon*
*before today.*

*And if you knew that,*
*you would have had time*
*to be ready for today.*

*But how would you be ready?*
*What would you have done?*
*Think about it now.*

*Would you have put things off,*
*as you always did,*
*promising tomorrow?*

*What becomes important?*
*what unimportant?*
*Focus—no time is left.*

*Did you tell Your Beloved*
*that you truly loved?*
*that you are thankful?*

*Reach out with your hands.*
*Bless Your Beloved.*
*God can flow through your hands now.*

*You have Power*
*you never had before.*
*Love and Peace are yours to give.*

*Let it flow like a river*
*I know how it feels...*
*because She blessed me.*

## My Reality

When My Beloved died
I felt most all of me *die*,
not much survived.

Inspiration, beauty, kindness,
love, eternal love,
all gone at once.

What is there left
when you lose all that?
There is nothing but part of me.

How can I build
a life with what remains?
All that is good left with her.

What is left me
is the only Reality
I have to work with.

Yet I must not withdraw,
become insensitive
to Life's Good, Life's Bad.

I guess it's my *Way*, my *challenge*.
It's *up* to me
to build up what's left.

What will I make of
this *Reality*
that is so diminished?

## Pain

Enter, join me—for
    I am friend to you.
It is only through my portals
    you can
        find yourself,
        grow anew.
Feel me, absorb me—
    here, put your hand
        into mine—tho'
I know it hurts you
    to feel me.
But I am your only Path,
    and you must take this Path.
Make me breath of your breath,
    heart of your heart,
And when I finally let you go,
    there will be a new You,
        in a New Life.
        Believe!

## Am I there?

I walked
into the Valley.
Behind me
all was light
and sweetness
and so beautiful.
But the door
was shut and
I could not go back.
And so...
I went into the Valley.
—all was
confusion,
darkness,
hidden pitfalls,
for two hundred days.
Now, finally
I can see
the end of the Valley
before me.
I must keep going.
I must find out
what is outside.
And will I meet
...myself?

# Days of the Wave

There are times,
   perhaps minutes,
   perhaps hours,
      when the Wave returns
      —the Wave of Grief.
The feeling of emptiness
   runs through our veins
      again...again...
   chooses its course,
   chooses its time,
      to remind us.
Once again we recall
   how much our Beloved
      did for us,
   made us what we became,
   brought wonders into
      our Life,
   worked miracles with Love,
   turned dark days into
      bright sunshine.
When Days of the Wave return,
   give your heart free rein,
   weep if you must,
   cry out your pain,
   fall on your knees,
   talk to your Beloved.
And the calm sea behind will
   come over you
   and soothe you,
      for God hears you.

# Section II

# Choosing Life

# The Choice

*Alone—and thinking—all is right.*
*But Alone Alone*
            *is different.*
*Thinking—*
        *when Alone Alone*
            *makes us aware*
                *—of the Void*
                *—of Emptiness*
                *—of the strange*
                    *space inside*
                    *that is empty.*

*Alone is temporary—*
        *perhaps even restful*
            *—a relief*
            *from a world*
                *not wanted.*
*Alone Alone*
        *—is to be without another present*
        *—is to know that it is*
            *unending*
        *—that the Spirit will weaken.*
*That is when you fear*
        *you won't make it back*
            *to where you were,*
        *and must take in hand*
            *the Life remaining.*
*It is yours,*
        *and the Choice to build or not*
            *is Yours.*

## Artist at Work

Life is a Painting
    emerging, trying
    to guide your hand.
Listen to your Life as it teaches
    for what Life does to you
    shapes, colors, and shades
        the eventual You.
Obstacles strengthen the sinews
    of the spirit,
problems challenge and frame
    the Face that will be yours.
In a painting of many colors
    and shades, Life must teach
       how to make those choices.
And among all that is taught,
    the hardest Life's teachings
      is that of Grief.
For then you are forced to
    take the brush in your hand,
    face up to what the painting
       must look like—
Your Life and your Painting
    One.

## When the Bell Calls

No tolling
   of a Bell
         can be called back.
Hearken, then—
   it gives its message
        but once—
When it tolls for Thee,
   it rings out thy Way.
Are you ready
   to hear?
        do you fear?
   turn a deaf ear?
The River of Life
   opens before you
        at the tolling
           of the Bell—
Fear its ringing
   and you—
        not awake—

# The Time of the Song

The Time of the Depths comes first.
Layers of depths never known,
    a time of tears, a time of penance,
    self-accusation, Self-punishment,
    awareness of mortality,
    awareness of inadequacy.
The next of Three
    brings drying tears,
    settling in of empty Silence,
    self-deception
        that Recovery is at hand.
    And in the Silence
        Pain still strikes,
        for Grieving is not yet o'er.
    Yet at the end of that Time
        a weight lifts,
        air flows to the lungs of the Mind,
        the Voice
            talking of Grief
                is strange to the Ear.
    The shattered Self is open.
The Time of the Song rushes in,
    flooding the Mind.
There is a new view of God,
    thankfulness—even for the Grief.
Miracles happen—
    if awake to them.
A New Song rings out,
    the sun shines.
The River of Life moves on,
    New Adventure awaits,
    calls out to be lived.
    Do not turn a deaf ear.

## A New Self, A New Life

I plumbed the depths,
depths...
I never knew, and while there
in those depths
God took my metal
and put it into a cauldron.
I burned,
I cried out,
"Why?"
I cried out,
"How much more?"
I cried out, "How long?"
And then I saw
God was re-shaping me inside...
deep inside.
My thought processes
were finding different channels.
My intellect felt a burning light,
and from that light truth flowed
and I was freer than ever I had been.
And I understood God's message
and when God said,
"Live your new Life
in the new Self I have given you.
You have done the work I gave
your old Self to do.
I have new work for you
but in a different Self,
a Self that is free, and open,
as I want all my people to be.
And fear not
the Life that will unfold.
I am with you.
Now go,
I love you."

## Be Glad In It

*Life giveth*
    *and Life*
          *taketh away.*
*But never takes*
    *without offering anew.*
*The Flow of Life*
    *is eternal...goes on...*
          *quietly at times,*
          *a tidal wave*
              *at others.*
*Awake and aware,*
    *New Life is there.*
*Grab it—*
    *it wants to take you*
          *with it.*
*Be Glad in it.*

## The Question

Where do I dwell?
   Am I where my Life
         was meant to be?
Living the Divine
   Adventure offered me?
Being My Life—
   accepting
            my own Being?
            my own Life?
The only Question
   worth asking.
Not did I
   attend—
   live where—
   make as much as—
   golf where—
Not any question
   anyone else asks—
Just one—
   am I living _my_ Life?

# Sail! Sail!

Hide not there,
    come!  Sign on!
        Follow your Love!
Experience the whole World
    made for you.
I tell you not
    that it is safe—
    for on all Seas
        terrible storms assault.
Yet the sun returns
    each time.
As does the rapture
    of a moonlit night.
Hard work it is
    to care for your ship,
    to repair damage
        after the storms.
But on the Sea
    you find your place
        in the Universe.
Sail where
    "no mariner has gone before."
And in the End,
    find only you
    are who you are.

# Section III

# Choosing Love

## It Is Love That Is Life

Fear no Love,
    for Love is the Great Commandment.
Not to love, out of fear,
    is to reject Life.
And that—
    that is the Sin of Sins.

It is Love
    that marries souls
    and unites.
It is Love
    that brings out sharing
    and turns on lights.
It is Love
    that raises beauty
    to the greatest heights.

Love, undisguised,
    cares more for the Beloved
    than for self.
Such love is pure
    and undefiled before all.
Admit such Love,
    'twill be your most perfect act.
For where Love is
    there God is.

# Knowing the Flow

'Twas magical
   —as tho'
       "my ship had come in"
          with precious cargo.
Of course,
   there was no ship
   —and no dock.
But she <u>was</u> present,
   standing there
      chatting
       —and beautiful.
I listened
   and joined in.
      Somehow I was drawn
        to want to know her.
   Why?
      Does anyone ever really
      know why?
All we know is
it is the Flow of Life
thru' the Mind.
The Spirit has its own way
and we don't know quite
—how it does it—
but it recognizes
its own Flow,
and will go with it
—the Flow to Bliss.

## In God's Time

Strange to speak
    of God and Time—
But we must
    if we are to understand—
            does God intervene
                    in the World of Time?
Why do we ask for help constantly
    as if He did?
We sense that
    "more things are wrought by prayer
    than this world dreams..."
How then?
    —through His timing of us.
When one is drawn to a Beloved—
    magically, mystically,
            miraculously—
    and the Beloved in the same way
            is drawn—
    Chemistry—Electricity—
Yet,
    Chemistry outside of God's Time
            is no chemistry—
    Electricity has no power
            outside of God's Time.
Love draws no response
    except
            in God's Time.
All else is Vanity, as said
    Ecclesiastes.

# How I Know

The moon speaks to me,
    the night air calls out.
The sun in the morning—
    even rain addresses me
        by name.
A bird flies by
    singing my name.

All of nature,
    the leaves in the trees—
        clouds in the sky.
All speak now
    for I am aware
        of them now—
understand their language.
Why this miracle?
    Do I now know
        the tongues of fire?
This experience—
    this adventure
        flowing through my mind—
It is there
    because She is
        here—
        now—
        with me—
And we both know why.

## Love's Plea

Waiting...
    living...
        longing...
Dreams and fantasies
    fulfillment
            of Yin and Yang
        together—One at last.
Love—
    fuels the engine
            that drives the world.
Imagination
    brings them together—
            the Lover,
            the Beloved.
Hearts float on air,
    Minds count Time
    and it weighs so...
Come, Anemone,
    Daughter of the Wind,
    whisk them together,
            Lover
            and
            Beloved.

## Dancing with You

The beauty that is you,
   I know,
      for I have danced
        with you.
The lovely shape of your face,
     the delightful form
       and grace
          of your body
        as you spin and twirl.
All that done by Nature
   took a million years
      to form a human being
        such as you.
But upon your face
   there is a light,
   and the smile
      of your heart
        shines through.
That was done solely by you.
   It took no million years,
      just a mere flash
        of your thought.

## Tomorrow

No more my lone figure
   under the moon,
        one shadow walking
            reflecting...
            praying...
            dreaming alone.
A New Love walks with me,
   dreams with me.
I now know
   ...Tomorrow is coming...
   a beautiful Love
        holds my heart.
When she is not with me,
   my eyes see her face,
   my ears hear her voice,
   my hand feels hers.
And I know
   I will have those
        Tomorrow.

# *Offering*

When I think of a river,
    I think of thee.
When I envision a wave
    upon a beach,
    I envision your beauty there.
When I walk at night,
    I walk holding your hand.
When I go to sleep
    it is with thee.
When I awake,
    I call your name.
All the day,
    in whatever I do
    I know it is for you.
You gave me this new life.
    Let me share it with you,
    offer it to you,
    while still I live it.
Love me in this new life.
    I must have it thus,
    my Offering to thee.

## God's Mystery Called Woman

How is a Woman's Love
    to be measured?
I touch my Beloved
    and know I have touched
    all of womankind.
She kisses me
    and I have been kissed
    by all women
    of all the millennia.
In her embrace
    I know the warmth
    of History's women.
I hear her voice
    and they have all
    spoken to me.
Still she is unique,
    there are none like her,
    there never were.
God's Mystery is there.
    One's Beloved is all Beloveds.
    Yet she is the only One.
    There can be no other
        to name your Beloved.
That is God's Mystery
    called Woman.

# SHE

*A graceful form*
    *glides toward me.*
*Beautiful of face,*
    *her smile fills the room*
        *with wonder.*
*She approaches nearer,*
    *I reach out my arms.*
*Into my embrace*
    *she warmly and*
        *willingly comes.*
*Entrancing perfume*
    *intoxicates.*
*The love in her arms*
    *tells me*
        *she belongs.*
*I am transported*
    *to the world*
        *created by the Great Lord*
            *of the River of Life*
        *for those who love,*
            *and with me is*
                *SHE.*

## Her Laugh

Life smiles,
   and my heart smiles,
      when she smiles.
But when She laughs,
   my whole world lights up.
Her laugh speaks
   the essence of Life.
It surrounds me, fills my ears,
        fills my heart,
        fills all the world
         round me,
        makes Life sweet
        and joyous.
She is the fullness of Woman,
   the Inspiration of Inspirations,
      a Creation only Divinity
        could have imagined.
The lovely Spirit within
   pours forth
      from her face,
       her voice,
       her smile,
       her laugh,
  pours forth
      and envelops me.
My mind surrenders to her Life,
   enthralled with the perfume
      of her laugh.

## Look On in Wonder

Through her Love,
    her warmth,
    her kind spirit,
Your Beloved shows you
    how God loves you.
She is the One
    who gives Life,
    as well as Love.
She is the One
    at risk for Loving,
    for surrendering,
    yet ne'er begrudges
    all she has given,
    never demands you give back
    what she surrenders,
    for what she surrenders
    is herself.
Look on in wonder then
    at the Gift of Love
    your Beloved offers.

## The Heart Ever Wakes

The Heart never sleeps,
    it centers on its love's desire.
The body craves for sleep,
    tho' the heart resists.
The mind yields to the body
        turning it off.
Irresistibly,
    the body takes itself and its mind
        into the darkness.
Now the heart seeks light,
    strives to find its love.
        Its way cut off, the gates closed,
        it searches for openings thru the mist
            of a sleeping mind
            inside a sleeping body.
As we all know,
    it will have its way, find an open gate,
    stir up the mind.
And now it can waken the whole body,
    fill the mind with the vision of
            its desire,
    Picture for it the beauty,
    the love, the Presence
        of the Beloved.
The Heart does not sleep,
    never ceases its messages
    that reveal Life's Loves.

## The Gift

The curtains part
to admit the Spring Wind.
Moonlight steals across the room.
My Beloved is not yet asleep.
I take her hand,
and she rises from her bed.
We stroll out the courtyard
to where the golden Waves
are playing on the beach.
Together, as one, we watch.
We are beyond Time.
We drink of the Wine of our Beings.
We are living the Love
given us by God,
and we weep in gratitude.

## I Love Thee Anew

At the first ray
    of stealthy light
    treading gently
    to my room,
    I love thee.
Thought begins
    to waken,
    stir up my soul,
    turn on my brain,
    I love thee.
My body turns and twists,
    muscles respond,
    legs unwind,
    toes uncurl,
    I love thee.
Covers off, no—
    covers back on!
    The radio snaps on—
    news, weather reports,
    I love thee.
Up, up, and away!
    Now all parts move,
    my brain functions,
    my soul greets the new day.
    And I know
        I love thee anew.

# Section IV

# Light on the River

## The Light

I happened to sail
   my river course
      to the bend
         where you were.
Why I stopped I know not,
   and why you were there
      you knew not.
Two Paths of Time,
   from 'round the Universe,
      crossed and
         lighted the night.
The power source
   was the Eternal,
      known o'er centuries
      by all who
         have realized
      the Presence of Love.
Letting the Presence
   pass through,
      take over the Spirit,
      become the Essence
         of Life—
That is the Light of the
   World.

# The Place of Light

A still place there is
   —deep inside—
that answers not
   to the world of Time,
a place of ideas,
   ideals,
   beautiful thoughts,
the source
   of our Imagination,
   of consolation,
   of warmth,
   of our knowing
      even before we know.
This still place
   is a passageway
      to eternal ideas,
      to Truth,
      to Faith,
      to the Courage to Be.
Blessed indeed are all
      who find it,
but for those who find it
      when there is no place
         else to go—
    its light
      is as the Sun
         at midday.

# The Fabric of Life

It is all only
    temporary—
and there are things
    you might want to keep
        as they are
    for all of Life.
But then
    part of what you were to do
        will not be done,
    and you were the one
        to do it.
The Fabric of the History
    of the Universe
        will be unfinished
        —forever—
When your cup runs over—
    and joy fills you
        it has limits
    and pours out your eyes.
When sadness makes a deep wound,
    it leaves you weeping,
    stunned, speechless.
Full Life will never
    be ought but a mixture.
Accept both—
    you will weep, I know—
but you will be living
    your part of
        the Fabric of Life.

## New Eyes, New Ears

There is a time
    when Truth can be known
    —the Truth about Life.
A door never seen opens...
    a Path unfolds—
        everywhere one finds
            new understanding.

The person you were
    is stripped of its shell—
        You made that shell,
            and it was not
    to be yours again.

When the shell came off your eyes,
    they saw, and
When it came off your ears,
    they heard.

You are bare now
    before God
        —you, Alone.
You got rid of your old God,
    you found now
        you could go to God
            —for the first time.

# Where? or Why?

Our River moves on,
nor all your paddling
or sweat
can call it back
to carve a different path.
We know we do not
control the River—
only swim.
Yet all of us
churning together
mark the course
—wondering—
What is this country?
you and I tumble through—
dividing walls,
smoothing hillsides...
We know we are here—doing—
but we can only wonder
—today—
Where are we going?
and Why?

# Water and Salt

*To the Sea*
*run all rivers,*
*and we—together—*
*are the streams,*
*for all the Ages*
*pouring...pouring...*
*rushing headlong*
*to the rivers.*
*And still,*
*the Sea is not filled.*
*The Sea, our Mother,*
*is generous with her Self,*
*gives back*
*as much as She receives.*
*We, the streams,*
*feed the rivers,*
*the rivers the Sea,*
*and the Sea...*
*completes*
*the Circle of Water*
*that is Life.*
*Salt of the Earth we are,*
*and Salt of the Sea become.*

## Mother of All

The Sea is all streams
    that pour across the Earth,
One massive Being,
    most powerful of living things.
Held by continents—
    none other could.
Fly over hastily, and
    never know the heavenly beauty,
    never quake mid the violent rages,
        when the Sea devours transgressors.
Incessant in its racing—
    everywhere at once,
    no part of Her ever
        in one place but a moment.
Yet there are times and places
    when the Sea is a still sheet
        of reflecting glass.
And if the moon be full,
    it is as day at night.
'Twas the Sea first gave birth
    —the Source of Life—
    and still all streams
    return to the Sea
    ...seeking...seeking...
    as infants to be joined to Her,
even as we seek...seek...our Source of Life.

## Seeing Now

Standing at the railing,
gazing across the waters,
focusing on both
    horizon and sky.
Now all is clear,
    you can see Eternity,
    know that your Now
        is eternal.
The Past is forgotten,
    the Future does not exist.
You feel, stirring within,
    full knowledge of all.
You are outside of Time.
Under foot the ship is
    carrying you to the
        Present on Earth.
Turn from the rail to the ship
    and you return to the Present-World,
        the sense of Eternity lost.
Stay, stay at the rail,
    it is a clear day and
        you can see your Eternity.

# Section V

# Images and Thoughts

# Learning

As I said,
   I know I am
   for I am thinking.
But why am I thinking?
   I didn't choose these thoughts.
They are as a stream
   coming to me
            and I use them
                  for a while.
Slowly it dawns on me—
   I am being taught—
            and that's how
                  I learn.
Thought without Learning
   is wasting precious inspiration.
It took me seven decades,
   but I know now
            my Teacher.

## Words Live

I write words,
        and—
                new life exists,
                thinks new thoughts,
                        shouts out for joy,
                                weeps out of deep sorrow,
        soars on wings of Love,
                speaks to my Beloved,
        calls out to my God,
                bends to inhale the aroma
                        of flowers ,
        looks at the heavens,
                and makes pictures
                        out of clouds.
Things that are not,
        my words bring into life.
They live on and on—
        I give them to my children,
                and they to theirs—and they—
Words—live forever
        —and forever create.
Write them—and
        fill the Universe
                with new life.

# Canyon

Cliffs and ledges—
    Altars in stone—
        spreading their aprons
          of gravel
          before them—
        the Beauty of Creation—
          and Creative Destruction.

Rim to Rim—
    and Depth following
        on Depth...
    all unending...
Telling their message
    without speaking—
        just being—
        for all to see,
    waiting for us to learn
        through our souls
        —spirit to spirit—
    we and they...
        are living...
          Eternity.

## Gardeners

We
      ...as the flowers, have a time to bloom.
And we are
      ...as flowers whose plants must be cultivated.
Without
      ...a gardener there will be no growth
                        and no flower.
Oh, I know
      there are wildflowers
               who must fight their enemies
                  on their own.
But we...
      with the help of our gardeners
               have progressed beyond the wild.
Who are they,
      these gardeners?
But who are they?
      The answer is simple—
                  anyone who truly loves us,
                  truly loves—
                        the self that we are.
Who wants us to
      complete all that is in us
               to be completed,
      say yes to that self inside,
      say yes to
               the life we find on our Way,
      say yes to
      Faith and Courage and Hope.
Those are our Gardeners.
      Seek them, they help us blossom,
               they work for God.

## Secret Garden

Gardens come in all sizes:
    tiny, mid-town, a veranda patch.
Everyman's size, with roses,
    jonquils, tomatoes.
Professional, Botanical, with
    everything known to man.
But the Secret One, buried
    deep, ours alone, unseen—
    the seed put there
        and not by us.
Its discovery our task,
    receiving it, cultivating it
    a question of love,
    its growth our Life Story.
And in that Garden learn to grow
    with another, be happy with the touch
    and caress of that flower,
        its perfume cast to the air about.
There is no garden just for you
    there must be another,
        or nothing grows
            in the Secret Garden.

# Water

Water,

it gave rise to all Life,
it sustains all Life.

Water, falling,
lights a city.

Water, still,
holds a ship afloat,
sends it on its way.

Water, angry,
may tear a ship apart.

Water cleanses, purifies.
It does all these things well.

All powerful is water,
yet the humblest of creatures.

Alone of all the things of Earth
    it unceasingly seeks
    the lowest place of Earth.

## The Light that Speaks

*Morning Light*
*    speaks to me.*
*At first*
*    it creeps across the room,*
*    stealthily approaching my bed.*
*Slowly, ever so slowly,*
*    it sprinkles itself*
*    over my eyes.*
*I open them warily*
*    seek to see who is there,*
*    shut them again,*
*    I don't need to know.*
*The light now emboldens,*
*    taps upon my brow.*
*I look again*
*    and say "not now."*
*A while passes,*
*    now impatient*
*    the light fairly shouts,*
*    my eyes are startled,*
*    I surrender*
*    and rise to greet the new day.*

# The Courage to Be

I thought I knew Him
    all these years.
It turns out I didn't,
    and only recently
    truly got to know Him,
    for the first time.
Oh, He watched me
    years ago,
    through a war alright,
    guided me,
    saved me,
    kept me alive.
He helped me stay well,
    take care of my family.
    I needed Him to raise
    those children.
Was it all coincidence
    that while I was preoccupied
    He spoke to my inner self?
Whatever it was,
    however He did it,
    I suddenly knew
    Faith is all,
    Religion is not,
    to live bravely as myself is all.
God had given me
    the Courage to Be,
    to live,
    and not fear Him.

## Images and Thoughts

They arise
from depths
out of the mists
of time and memory.
Pictures at an Exhibition—
visions, fantasies
but all
true Life.
Dreams they are not,
but the stuff
of dreams
they are.
They cannot be turned off,
remain inside
forever—
Life and Love,
beautiful and wonderful
painful and hurtful,
pleasant and happy,
all now
images and thoughts,
irremovable,
unstoppable,
eternal.

# The World Hidden

*Where is the real, the clean,*
*the beautiful*
*of all the world?*
*Where can we find*
*the true, the good*
*Moslem, Buddhist, Jew.*
*Irish, Lebanese, Colombian?*
*Other peoples,*
*other cultures,*
*they are shown to us*
*when rioting,*
*shooting, killing.*
*How can we believe*
*they and we are all one?*
*What is inside*
*the world*
*that is hidden from us?*
*When we know that,*
*then we can believe*
*we can*
*love one another,*
*live in peace,*
*know we are one.*

## *You Only Have to Reach Out*

*We were given the great Gift of Life.*
*Contemplate it if you can*
*non-existence.*
*Now realize values, infinite in scope,*
*given you, for you lived.*
*Whatever happened, you lived it.*
*Your fears, your deeds, your pains, joys,*
*your whole Way through Life.*

*And did you love?*
*You were blessed.*
*Were you loved in return?*
*Then you were blessed beyond measure.*
*You truly lived!*

*To touch the Face of God*
*we must have loved,*
*for that is the whole of the message*
*we were given— to love those*
*we find on our Way.*
*That is our Life.*

*Reach out now*
*to touch those*
*before you.*
*That is to touch*
*the Face of God.*

## Battlefield Truth

*In the telling of all Myths by all Peoples,*
*the Pattern is the same—*
*the story of the Passage, the Journey,*
*of a Man or Woman*
*from which Journey we take Spiritual Solace,*
*the explanation of Life,*
*a Guide for our own Passage.*
*In all we see,*
*the Adventure of a Goddess,*
*the Battles of a God,*
*and in them our own trials*
*and follies,*
*the Source of our own Hope.*
*In my own tale,*
*like a Man of a Myth,*
*I went out to my War,*
*and learned the Truth of a Battlefield—*
*Everyone who lives through those days*
*has lived on others' Deaths.*
*That is the Guilt and Truth*
*of the Battlefield.*
*The Deaths that saved us,*
*the Deaths we caused—*
*All were part of the same Spirit*
*as Ourselves.*
*And we came to know the Hurt,*
*because we all*
*belonged together*
*in One Universal Life!*
*And we needed afterward*
*to be cleansed—*
*but no one cleansed us!*

# Weaving

We look back
—finally—
examine Life,
and discover
there was a Pattern
—the Fabric is whole—
How was this woven?
Did we really—?
We acted—
but the Pattern?
Didn't we just
deal with what we found
across our Path?
in our Path?
The Whole we did not see
till now.
All we are, all we
came to be—
woven into one Pattern.
Yet each one of us also wove,
uniting with other patterns
here, dismissing there,
and each in turn
wove.
All of us made Patterns
together.
But the Whole,
the Whole—
That required—
a Master Weaver.

# Section V

# China

# Four Seasons in China

Hot, steamy Shanghai of Summer,
    the struggling millions,
    foul-smelling water,
    mosquitoes and cockroaches
    ...and dirt.
Autumn and Shanghai
    slowly cooling,
    cloudy days increasing,
    filth growing in the air.
Winter, people without heat
    in cold and windy Shanghai,
    damp and penetrating,
    coal dust filling lungs,
    streets laden with spit.
Finally, with the first new moon
    of the New Year approaching,
off to Kun-ming:
Sunshine and clear air,
warmth,
flowers,
spring-time clothing,
happier people,
outdoor markets,
a freeing of the Spirit.
The West Hills,
rest spots clinging
to perches like eagle nests.
Temples, ponds,
paintings, and Buddhas.

A gathering of Fulbright Professors
from all round China.
The Stone Forest, rickety buses,
The Burma Road, denuded hills.
The many independent
nationality peoples of China,
who cared nothing for Beijing.
Creative people
—with strange foods.
A glorious, healthful week,
and the last such we would know.
The Fourth Season lay ahead,
Spring would bring
the massacre of our students
who loved China and Freedom.

Four Seasons—and the Fourth filled
with the white flowers of Death.

## Slaughter in the Night*

In the darkness
of early morning,
while the people slept,
tanks rolled their way
through their tents,
grinding, grinding
like huge meat machines.
Undeserved deaths,
blood-letting troops,
satanic government!
May there be a Hell
for them!
This was not war.
War is against an enemy.
This was murder...
planned, cold-blooded murder
...of their own people.
There is evil in the world,
and it is here...now...
in China.
How far will it go—
this slaughter in the night?

*June 3-4, 1989, written that morning.

# The River of Life*

Come, come to the River —
    not when it is still,
    but rushing headlong.
Swim in its currents,
    toss in its eddies.
Taste of its waters,
    it is Life that is the torrent.

Humanity is there
    tempest toss'd,
    swimming frantically.
Where it is going
    none of us knows.

But we do know this:
    the River knows.
It is the River of Life
    in the world.
Its channel is set,
    its feeding streams pour
    the Plan of Life
    into its depths.

Now and then
    it floods its banks,
    people are caught
    in its currents,
        but they are not lost
          forever.

*When the Rains of Freedom*
        *fill our valleys,*
                *Power dams the stream,*
        *but it will return*
                *to flood again.*

*There is no holding back*
        *The River of Life...*

* *written flying home from China after Tienanmen.*